LIFT-THE-FLAP
ABC

Illustrated by Jim Hodgson

If you look at the picture on each page then lift the flap, you will discover another object that begins with the same letter. Now look at each picture again. How many other things can you find that begin with the same letter?

TEMPLAR

BCDEFGHIJKLMNOPQRSTUVWXYZ.

NOAH 1

and a
is for...

B is for Beach

and b is for...

C is for Circus

and c is for...

E is for Elephant

and e is for...

F is for Farm

and f is for...

G is for Gate

and g is for...

H is for Horse   and h is for...

I is for Ice

and i is for...

J is for Jungle

and j
is for...

K is for Kangaroo
and k is for...

L is for Lion

and I is for...

N is for Night

and n is for...

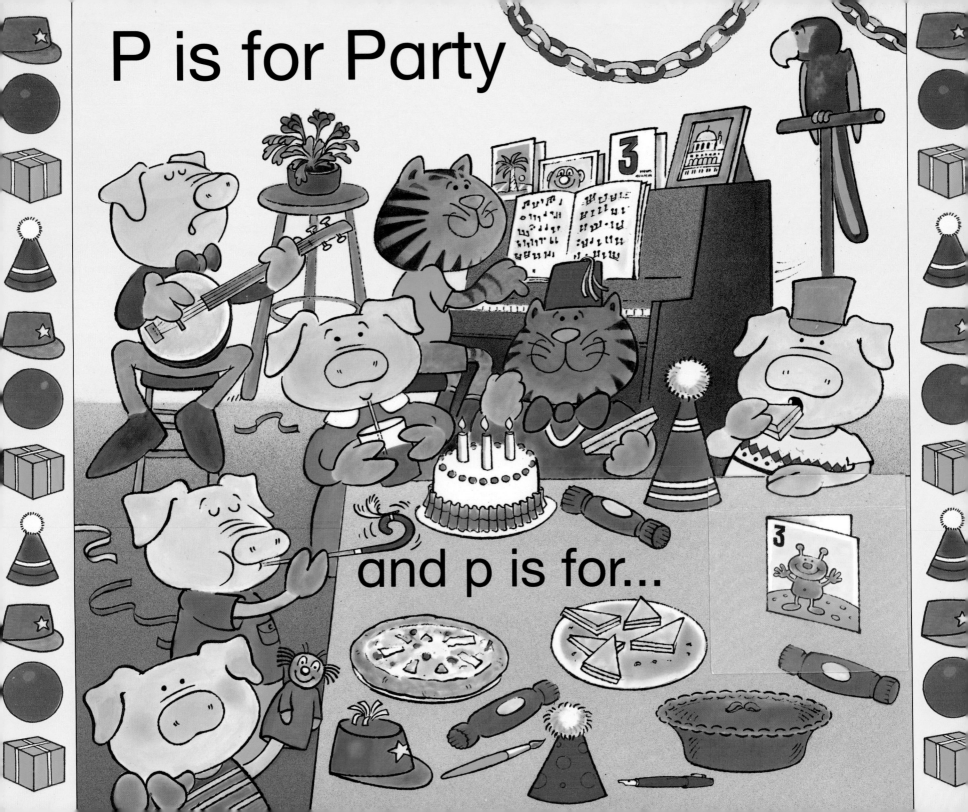

P is for Party

and p is for...

Q is for Quilt

R is for River

and r is for...

V is for Vet

and v is for...

PLEASE WAIT HERE

X is for Xmas

(this word is often used to shorten Christmas)

Y is for Yak and y is for...

Z is for Zoo

PLEASE
DON'T FEED
THE ANIMALS

BEARS

HIPPOS
+
CROCODILES